BEHAVIOR

GUIDANCE

for
INFANTS and
TODDLERS

BEHAVIOR GUIDANCE
for
INFANTS and
TODDLERS

ALICE STERLING HONIG, Ph.D.

SOUTHERN EARLY CHILDHOOD ASSOCIATION

7107 W. 12th St., Ste. 102 • Little Rock, AR 72204
P.O. Box 55930 • Little Rock, AR 72215-5930
Office: 501-663-0353 • FAX: 501-663-2114

Second Printing

The names of all children and families in this book have been changed to protect their privacy.

The Southern Early Childhood Association provides a variety of publications, videos, and symposia for teachers and care givers of young children. For more information about our services, write, call, or e-mail us at SECA@aristotle.net or visit us on the Internet at www.seca50.org.

SECA makes every effort to assure that developmentally appropriate practices and cultural diversity are depicted throughout our publications, products, and materials. The opinions expressed in this book, however, are those of the author(s) and not necessarily of SECA and/or its affiliates.

ISBN 0-942388-18-6

Printed in the United States of America
by A.C.H. Graphics   tel. 1-501-753-6113

CONTENTS

INTRODUCTION

WHAT IS MISBEHAVIOR FOR BABIES?

Crying is a powerful tool that babies use to signal an immediate need for help and relief. Crying is an appropriate behavior that helps infants get their basic physical and emotional needs met. If a baby cries, the adult may interpret that action as

The responsive caregiver attends to the baby's needs.

"disturbing my sleep" or "doing it just to annoy me." Many actions of babies that parents and caregivers find exasperating are NOT intentional misbehaviors. However, an infant has few tools to urgently request that care be given. When a baby cries, the responsive, attuned caregiver interprets the signal of the cry as a way of communicating a need. The caregiver then searches for ways to relieve the infant's distress. The responsive caregiver understands that the baby is trying with a limited communication repertoire to call for help.

During the first year of life, prompt attentiveness to crying followed by attempts to interpret correctly and tune into the infant's signalled needs will lead to secure attachment to the caregiver. This secure attachment between the

7

infant and the caregiver is the single most powerful means to ensure later compliance and cooperation as the baby becomes mobile and moves into toddlerhood. Secure attachment gives a baby the courage to cope with caregiver requests and tasks.

Some developmental tasks are more difficult to accomplish than others. Learning to eat neatly with a utensil, or learning to poop in a potty rather than diapers, and learning to share toys with others are difficult developmental tasks for babies and toddlers. All children mature at different rates so some babies learn such skills earlier than others.

Photo: Jan Wilson

Learning to feed one's self neatly with a utensil is an important task.

Some infants need far more time to develop control over their muscles or to gain the motivation needed to comply with adult wishes. Toddlers do not always follow adult schedules for toilet training. Males often need an extra year or more to learn to control sphincter muscles and urinate in a given place at a given time. An adult who demands toilet use too early or too sternly without regard for the developmental readiness of the child may face unhappy clashes over "accidents." Toddlers who have toileting accidents are not "disobedient." They may want to respond to adult pressure for more mature behaviors, but are unable to organize such coordinated response patterns. Coercive adult responses to a child who is not developmentally ready to comply increases the chances for resentful and defiant behavior from that child.

Learning some developmental tasks requires a great deal of adult assistance. Empathy and loving support from the caregiver will help this learning process be positive for both the child and the caregiver. Some social skills are harder to master because the physiological needs of the infant at that stage are greater than his ability to understand and comply with adult rules. For example, Caroline might bite Eric because her gums are swollen and itchy. Caroline is biting to relieve a physical need; however being bitten is no fun for Eric.

The first lesson for determining whether a behavior is indeed a misbehavior is to examine accurately the baby's ability to understand and to carry out an adult's wishes.

For example, Justin's mother props a bottle of juice in his crib and leaves him to drink it. Justin loosens the cap and spills juice all over himself and his bed. Justin starts to cry. Nothing happens. Justin cries and screams more loudly. His mother comes into the room and sees the wet crib and the juice all over Justin. Faced with another clean up job, she slaps him and screams, "You are so bad! You've been asking for it, all day! All I do is clean up after you."

By accusing the baby of misbehavior, Justin's mother is using a Freudian defense mechanism called "projection of evil." Parents and caregivers must learn to have realistic expectations in terms of infant levels of understanding and competence. Otherwise, misbehavior becomes anything the adult doesn't like or finds a nuisance.

What is misbehavior? **Misbehavior is a deliberate action contrary to adult rules when a child fully understands those rules, and has the capacity to obey them mentally, emotionally, and physically.** Therefore, the first lesson for guiding an infant toward self-control and cooperation is to remember the developmental stage and the physical needs of the baby.

Time tables for developmental accomplishments differ since each person is unique. Remember that some behaviors that make adults uncomfortable are in reality appropriate for the developmental age of the child. For example, a toddler who promptly answers, "NO" to everything is really just experiencing a normal developmental stage. A two year old who puts his/her hands into his/her pants to pat genitals while intently concentrating on the story you are reading may make you feel uncomfortable. Nevertheless, these are not misbehaviors. These behaviors are entirely appropriate for the child's age and stage.

Before labeling these actions as misbehaviors, think more deeply how your own family reacted to you when you were a "NO" saying toddler, or your own personal history of being chastised when you were young. Sometimes difficulties with parents or caregivers in our own past interferes with professional judgment about what is normal stage-specific behavior rather than "bad" behavior.

DISCIPLINE VS. PUNISHMENT

Discipline means to teach

Discipline means to teach. Think of long-term goals as the most important ones. The goal of the adult is not just to coerce the child into short term compliance. The ultimate goal of discipline is to rear self-regulated children so that later on they can control their own behaviors, even when a parent or a teacher is not in the room.

Punishment, such as shaming, spanking, locking a child in a closet, or harshly scolding and ridiculing, teaches children fear and defiance. Punishment destroys self esteem. Punishment may relieve an angry adult, but it rarely teaches the child any social lessons. Punishment limits long-term self control, which is the ultimate goal of discipline. Frequently punished children may learn to be "good" while adults are watching. However, they also learn to be ashamed of their bodies and their actions. They learn to lie, to accuse others, to pretend, and to build up angers and sullen rages against all adults, including caregivers.

POSITIVE DISCIPLINE TECHNIQUES WITH BABIES

PREVENTION: THE OPTIMAL DISCIPLINE TECHNIQUE

Many actions that are interpreted as misbehaviors occur because adults fail to recognize infant signals. Tiredness, overstimulation, and unfamiliar surroundings overwhelm infants and toddlers. The toddler who throws a temper tantrum in the midst of a family holiday gathering when told that she must go up to bed, is unable to cope with tiredness. The stress of the special event is also difficult for her to process. Overtired, she falls into a tantrum. Raging with tears, she protests that she wants to stay downstairs with everyone. The parent or caregiver can avoid such unpleasant scenes by using a few prevention techniques. First, give the toddler plenty of advance notice that soon she will have to leave the gathering. Next, allow her time to get into pajamas, and to kiss everyone good night. Finally, have a favorite family adult come up and sing an extra song or read her a story. These steps still make the child feel involved with the celebration and allow her time to make the transition to going to bed. Planning a longer nap in the afternoon when you know a child will be up later in the evening may also prevent behaviors which result from being overly tired.

Avoid power struggles with toddlers. Toddlers are wrestling with power issues and striving to test the limits of their ability to control others. According to Eriksonian theory, in the second and third year of life children are trying to assert willfulness, and initiate their own ideas. While at the same time, adults are often trying to "civilize" and "train" them. In an effort to "train" children, adults often use coercive methods that lead to shame and rage. In addition, these methods reinforce doubts toddlers have about their own intrinsic worth and capabilities.

Advance adult planning often avoids **misbehaviors** which result in a child being scolded or punished. Putting caps on wall plugs makes it impossible for a creeping baby to poke a finger into a plug. Putting a heavy chair in front of a wobbly floor lamp prevents a baby from creeping up, and yanking on the lamp cord. A childcare worker must remember to remove the partially-filled vegetable soup bowl from a high chair tray before cleaning up the baby's face and hands. Otherwise, as the worker moves on to clean up another child, the "clean," baby can easily and gracefully dump the remaining soup on herself. Your advance planning avoids messes and disputes.

Learning to predict how a child might react to a situation can help buffer an adult against irritated feelings. Learn how to make better predictions so you can "head off at the pass" behaviors that would otherwise lead to chastisement. Try to perceive the situation from a baby's point of view. The child is not trying to create an aggravating extra mess. She is finished with lunch and dumping the bowl seems an interesting experiment. Even if vegetable soup is hard to get out of the hair, Remember that babies are creative. Babies try new experiences with materials in order to figure out how objects work. Infants and toddlers cannot understand the future effect of an action very precisely. Your perceptive realizations of how the situation seems to the baby will prevent many negative scenarios and surely cut down on cleanups.

Timing is often critical in prevention of frustration on the part of the adult. If a baby wakes several times at night, an exhausted parent may become resentful. The parent could try moving the baby's late night nursing closer to the parental bed time. Then the baby may only wake for one more feeding before morning, rather than several. A latch installed high up on the bathroom door is more effective than the threats of a "spanking" for the newly mobile and curious toddler who decides to explore the

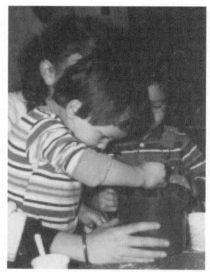

Photo: Subjects and Predicates
Babies try new experiences with materials in order to figure out how objects work.

results of dumping all her toys into the toilet. The latch is a more practical prevention technique than constant scolding.

SECURE ATTACHMENT: NURTURING THE SECRET INGREDIENT THAT GIVES BABIES THE COURAGE TO COPE

Babies whose caregivers have been responsive to their needs in the early months of their lives are far more likely to attend to the warnings or requests of caregivers later.

The following adult behaviors promote secure attachment and predict more cooperativeness and compliance with adults years later:

1) Hold infants tenderly in your arms for nursing with breast or bottle. Feed them leisurely. Tune in to infant cues. Adjust your body posture to help an infant who needs to burp or change position while feeding.

2) Give the infant a chance to be on a warm, safe floor area to practice pushing up and wiggling his limbs freely.

3) Respond promptly but not anxiously to distress signals and provide appropriate comforts, depending on the problem. Sometimes the problem requires rescuing a child from a tight situation and reassuring her with a hug.

4) Give baby your personalized, focused attention.

USE CALM TONES AND CARESSES

Photo: Francis Wardle

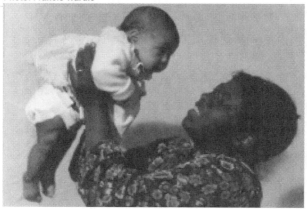

Hold a young baby **en face** *position*

Babies are born with the ability to cooperate with adult requests that they calm down. Use low soothing repetitive voice tones and cuddling to reassure an upset baby that he will be all right. Also, hold a young baby in *en face* position. That is, support both bottom and head firmly while you hold baby about 12 inches from your face. In that position, baby will often turn his head to find your eyes. The baby manages to pull himself together just by focusing on your reassuring face and listening to your soothing voice. Of course, if the baby is hungry, nursing is a far better solution than a low reassuring voice. But suppose the baby has been suddenly awakened by a loud noise, or picked up and taken to a different room. Sudden change is upsetting to the infant. Repeated reassurances in loving tones may well help an infant to organize her own self-control and find her own fist and suck on it in order to soothe herself.

Use your body and voice to calm an upset infant. Hold a baby closely in your arms and gently sway back and forth. Firm cheek-to-cheek holding is especially soothing for "tactile defensive" infants, who respond with irritability to light skin touches. Use your caressing voice tones to help the baby hold together emotionally so she can organize all the bewildering sensations that are throwing her equilibrium off at the moment.

Photo: Nancy P. Alexander

Babies thrive in the aura of loving voice tones.

Use caressing voice tones while diapering or bathing a little one. Babies thrive in the aura of loving voice tones. On a changing table, a 17 month old kicks his legs and gurgles with delight hearing the pleasure in the caregiver's voice tones. The caregiver enlists the baby's cooperation with diaper changing through loving cooing, turn-taking talk, and cheerful explanations of the diapering process. Admire vocally how handsome the baby looks, how deliciously dimpled and kissable is each waving finger.

Listen for the tone of your own voice. Tight adult voice tones increase infant tension. Angry cold tones make babies fearful. When you need to be very serious, if a dangerous situation is at hand, lower your voice tones. Remain calm, but mean every word you say as you explain about danger to a toddler.

Voice tones are especially important when a toddler is having a tantrum and is out of control. Be there to support the child. Hold her firmly so flailing limbs do not hurt you. Harsh panicky adult tones, sharp criticism of the tantrum, hysteria creeping into the adult voice are all signals to the toddler that the adult too, is sliding out of control. The tantrum can even grow worse as the child responds to the hysteria or harsh voice of the adult. Keep trying through reassuring words to let an out-of-control child know you will keep him safe. By remaining calm you are giving the child the message that you will help him get back into control. Your actions can demonstrate that you are ready to listen when he is ready to tell you about what happened. Acknowledge how upset he is. Let the child know you are there for him by the way in which you control your voice tones and actions as you hold him securely.

REFRAME "NAUGHTY" BEHAVIORS

Photo: Nancy P. Alexander

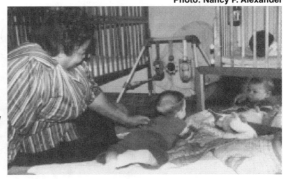

The astute caregiver reframes what looks like misbehavior and refocuses the child's behavior.

The astute caregiver reframes what looks like "misbehavior." The infant who squashes a piece of bread in his hand as he pushes the bread into a cup of milk on his high chair table is not deliberately trying to make a mess. He is just trying to understand the sensory experience. He is experimenting with textures and objects. He is trying to understand the transformation of the solid bread into the soggy dripping mess he has pulled from his cup. "Reframing" is a useful caregiver technique. The caring adult thinks about the meaning of the experience from the baby's point of view. The adult figures out what the baby is experiencing and learning by the "mess" he just made. The caregiver can then decide if she or he wishes to provide other ways in which the baby can feel squashy sensuous materials (try cornstarch glop) without having a soggy food mess to clean up. Or perhaps, after looking at the situation from the child's point of view, the adult will decide that the soggy bread is fine as a learning experience, especially if baby then pops the mess into his mouth and enjoys eating it.

FOCUS BABY'S ATTENTION BEFORE ASKING FOR ACTION

Photo: Francis Wardle
Focus baby's attention before asking for action.

Toddlers are busy folks. They are newly mobile and need to be on the go. Often it is even difficult to get them to lie still for a diaper change. They are not being defiant, instead they are motivated to practice their walking. They are excited to see what they can do with this giddy, wonderful verticality they are trying to master in space. If you want a toddler to do something, it is best to get his attention first. "Look! See the yellow ball! Roll the ball to papa!" gets more cooperation than simply urging baby to "roll the ball."

First, get the baby to focus on what you want him to notice. Next, ask for an action that is familiar and preferred. This sequence, which alerts the baby into attentiveness first, has a better chance of succeeding in capturing baby's interest in the activity you are suggesting.

This technique works well if the baby is frustrated with a difficult toy and is ready to hurl it without regard for a nearby peer. Suppose that the baby is having trouble learning to manage the Jack-in-the-box toy. If you focus his attention first on pushing down the top or on how he can turn the crank on the toy, then he may get the hang of coordinating the actions required to enjoy mastering the Jack-in-the-box.

GESTURES ADD SUPPORT AND HELP DECREASE FRUSTRATION

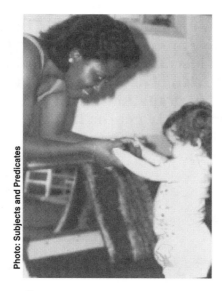

Gestural supports help toddlers achieve a sense of independence.

Some activities are quite difficult for a young toddler to master. Stacking boxes can be frustrating to put together. In order to prevent a child from giving up angrily or sweeping toy pieces abruptly off a table, try steadying the lower pieces of the stacking toy. Provide unobtrusive supports for a small child's arm and elbow. Unobtrusive bodily supports go far toward helping a toddler persist at a difficult task, such as nesting or stacking boxes. At the same time, the toddler feels in control of the activity. Toddlers are particularly sensitive to issues of control. Thus, the use of gestural supports should be low-key so that the toddler feels she is accomplishing the task on her own for the most part. As the child becomes more proficient at the task, your supports can be decreased.

SCULPT REQUIRED TASKS INTO GAMES

Toddlers enjoy water play.

Infants and toddlers are great copycats. They like to imitate each other, and they like to imitate adults. Seated waiting for dinner in a group care situation, one baby bangs both hands on the table. Then the rest of the babies giggle and bang their hands on the table. Because babies are great imitators, they will imitate many caregiver behaviors. They may try to use a rag to clean up a table or pretend to read a book with a singsong babble. Integrate helping into all room chores. Encourage toddlers to help you clear off plastic and paper lunch plates. Let them stand on a safe stool and wash dishes in sudsy water. Toddlers love "water play!"

Let them help you fold and put away laundry. Laundry sorting helps build their cognitive categorization abilities. Some socks or towels are little. Some are big. Doing simple chores alongside a special adult confirms for toddlers that they are important persons and helpers in a family or in a childcare setting. Each time toddlers participate at their level in daily routine chores, they are learning the rules of the activity, the sequences, and the process. In addition, they are learning basic rules of socialization and the value of participation in routine activities. Putting away blocks or cars, setting the table for snack, and using soapy sponges to wipe off the work tables, are good opportunities for enjoyable game-like activity rather than required chores which are "imposed" on toddlers.

AFFIRM A CHILD'S EFFORTS

Babies cannot perfect a new skill at first try. Almost any new skill requires lots of practice and entails lots of spills and sprawls in the floor. If an infant or toddler is striving to learn a new skill, encourage early tries in a low-key way. A toddler feels frustrated as she tries to solve a puzzle that is unfamiliar. For example, suppose Eva were trying to solve a puzzle of a "Puppy On

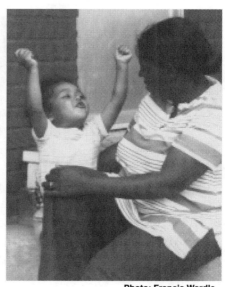

Photo: Francis Wardle
Affirm a child's effort.

The Grass." Remark with quiet appreciation "Eva, you are trying really hard to fit the puzzle pieces in the board. You are turning the pieces around. You are trying to notice where the green pieces fit with other green pieces to make the grass. You are a hard worker!" Some children need more encouragement than others. Some need to have their efforts validated by an empathic, nurturing adult. Toddlers may get angry if you help; other times they get frustrated and mad if you do not help!

Toddlerhood is not an easy stage. Most toddlers appreciate a quiet affirmation of their hard working efforts, even if at the moment they are not successful.

REWARD DESIRED BEHAVIORS CONTINGENTLY: DO NOT OVERPRAISE

Photo: Nancy P. Alexander

Appreciate compliant gestures.

Appreciate compliant gestures. When a baby does something which is appropriate and shows some effects of your socialization efforts then appreciate the baby's compliant gestures. If you finish washing a 14 month old, pat her dry, and start to put on her shirt, note that she has put up her right arm for you to dress. Do not ignore this helpful action and start to put the shirt sleeve on the other arm first. Contingent, prompt reinforcement right after a child's action increases the chance that the desirable behavior will recur more frequently. Many adults believe that discipline means only chastising or correcting undesirable behaviors. **Positive discipline includes "building up" the behaviors you do want to see.** Positive prompt reinforcement, that is not overly gushing, is likely to result in a child trying further to work hard and persist at a difficult task. Children work not only for the intrinsic satisfaction of the task, but also to gain the approval of their special intimate caregivers. Pride in their own accomplishments is important to children. However, feeling the admiration of a loved and loving adult is also important.

STATE AND RESTATE CLEAR SIMPLE RULES AND EXPLANATIONS

Toddlers need to know rules for harmonious group behavior, whether in a household or in a childcare facility. They need caregivers to restate rules many times. Adult rules may not make conceptual sense to babies. They do not have adult standards of the importance of a clean orderly environment. If they have learned to climb, they may feel victorious about climbing up on a low

Photo: Nancy P. Alexander
Explain rules calmly.

table. A rule that seems eminently reasonable to adults, from the point of view of cleanliness and safety, may seem like an unfair and bewildering restriction on baby's freedom to explore the environment. Certain adult rules are important to protect very young children. State these rules calmly. Be prepared to restate them firmly and also act to reinforce the rules through body language. "Feet belong on the floor. You cannot stand up on the table, Daniel" needs to be reinforced gently and firmly by lifting Daniel down, and restating the rule. A simple explanation such as "I don't want you to fall and get hurt" may or may not be understood by a toddler.

Be sure that you think through which rules are absolutely essential and which rules simply put a burden on the budding cognitive capacity of infants and toddlers. "Gently, honey. I need my eyeglasses to stay on my face," repeated cheerfully time after time as you extricate your glasses from the exploring affectionate fingers of the 10-month-old in your arms may eventually make sense to the baby.

LABEL DESIRABLE BEHAVIORS: PROVIDE POSITIVE ATTRIBUTIONS

Affirm your faith in infants by ascribing positive motivations and positive feelings to their behaviors. If one toddler sees another fall down hard and then goes over to pick up the body of the protesting peer, you could say, "Ben, you are really trying to help Ora get up. She fell down. You want to help her up. Thank you for caring and trying to help. But Ora wants to try to get up by herself. Let's see if she can manage." If a toddler pats a cat gently, tell him how gently he patted the cat. He is a gentle person with animals. He is kind to the cat. If a toddler takes her soiled tissue after you wipe her nose and actually runs to put it in the trash can when asked, affirm that she is a big helper. You appreciate her helping.

If a child interacts with an animal, appropriately affirm his actions.

Giving children positive attributes identifies their behaviors as helpful, kind, sharing, and patient. Children need to hear the words for positive attributions far more than the negative disciplinary or punitive words they often hear from adults chastising them for behaviors that irritate or anger the adults.

ARRANGE THE ENVIRONMENT THOUGHTFULLY TO PROMOTE PEACEFULNESS

Photo: Francis Wardle

Children need toys they can act upon.

Room arrangements can facilitate peaceful, prosocial interactions or lead to more antagonistic peer conflicts. These antagonistic behaviors impel adults to disapprove with words and actions. A block area should be large enough so that toddlers are not crowded. There should be enough large building blocks for several children to feel comfortable about building at the same time. Crowding promotes interpersonal aggression among very young children.

Some environments are overstimulating for infants. They are cluttered, noisy and crowded. Babies may react by hitting, biting, or whining. Look at your environment. Is it conducive to peaceful individual or peer play? Are there cushions on the floor where an overstressed baby can creep or toddle in order to snuggle down and recoup emotionally?

Too sterile or bare an environment can also lead to irritability. Babies and toddlers need enough toys, a variety of textures, and safe crawling spaces. In addition, young children need toys that do something when acted upon (such as squeak toys, windup toys, busy boxes, and pull toys). These types of toys satisfy a child's urges to explore and learn. An interesting environment provides a carefully planned mixture of sensory and motor development opportunities to engage very young children. Uninteresting, barren rooms are easier to keep clean. But they do not offer opportunities for a baby to play and learn safely at a level congruent with his capabilities. Both overstimulating and understimulating environments lead to behaviors that are perceived by adults as "misbehaviors."

MODEL THE BEHAVIORS YOU WANT TO SEE IN CHILDREN

Model self control, kindness, cooperation, courtesy, and patience. Adults are powerful role models for young children. Well before two years, babies whose parents are abusive learn to lash out with aggressive hitting and scratching. Adults often show inappropriate "amusement" when a toddler imitates their angry shouted curses or swaggering adult aggressive actions.

Photo: Nancy P. Alexander
Model the behaviors you want to see in children.

When you want young children to obey reasonable rules and comply with reasonable requests for cooperative play, think about the kinds of prosocial modeling you provide daily. In one toddler classroom, a peer bent down and tried hard to twist his friend's sneaker laces around and around. He did not know how to tie laces. However, he had so often seen Mr. Jonathan, his caregiver, bend down gently and helpfully to tie toddler laces so that a child would not stumble and fall. The boy imitated Mr. Jonathan's nurturing ways by trying to tie his friend's flopping laces.

If you wish toddlers to be patient as you get each one dressed to go outdoors on a snowy day, then be sure to model patience in your voice when you are waiting for all the toddlers to get on the rug at reading time and settle down for a story.

34

Be patient with the slow pace of infant/toddler socialization learning. Babies become ready to learn socialization requirements at very different times. Some can say "ta-ta" for "thank you" by 18 months. Some babies use a spoon neatly long before two years. Others are so impatient for food that they scoop it up with their fingers if lunch is delayed even by a few minutes.

Adults who understand how hard it is to learn neatness or impulse control will not be overly prone to jump in and do something for a child trying on his own, nor will they accuse the child of making a mess. Babies learn by trial and error. They act on materials over and over. Learning to pour from a teapot into a small cup takes so much effort that Leyvon's tongue is thrust out as he concentrates carefully on pouring. Yet he may still spill a good deal of water. Have a sponge handy. He is not naughty. He is working on pouring skills.

A caregiver murmurs "You're making me nervous" as a baby tips the training cup filled with milk too far and milk dribbles all over his bib. Patience goes a long way in helping the child master this new skill. Wrist control is built slowly and is often not securely in place until 18 months. The baby is not "misbehaving." He is learning to use the muscles that eventually will result in eating neatly.

Caregivers who learn infant ages and stages as well as normative timetables and "windows" for achieving normal developmental milestones can better assess a baby's readiness for learning new tasks including socialization skills.

QUALITY GROUP CARE PROMOTES INFANT/ TODDLER COOPERATION

Research shows that infants and toddlers who receive high quality care are more compliant with teacher requests and are more likely to get along peacefully with one another.

The following are strong indicators of high quality care:

Fewer than four babies per caregiver.

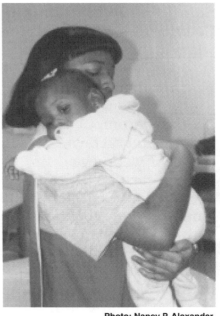

Photo: Nancy P. Alexander

Small group size.

Photo: Nancy P. Alexander

Photo: Nancy P. Alexander

Well trained caregivers, who have taken many courses and workshops in infant/toddler development.

Stability of staff with low turnover, so that babies can count on consistent care from beloved caregivers.

Photo: Nancy P. Alexander

When toddlers are moved *with* familiar peers to an older age group, this lessens distress and acting out at this transition time.

Photo: Nancy P. Alexander

Photo: Nancy P. Alexander

Quality care makes a difference in increasing cooperation and peaceful relationships among children.

KEEP ROUTINES PREDICTABLE AND COMFORTABLE

Babies are very routine oriented. It takes time for them to digest new experiences, new ways of holding, new feeding experiences, and new expectations for more mature behaviors. They thrive when they can make sense of daily rhythms, persons, and ways of being nurtured. The more calm and predictable the daily rhythms of

Photo: Nancy P. Alexander

Babies are very routine oriented.

their lives are, the more peacefully they will react, and the more readily they will cooperate. Regularity does not mean rigidity. Flexibility that is carried out within the context of nurturing, meaningful daily experiences can be cognitively and emotionally enriching. Stability of care from responsive, attuned caregivers best guarantees this predictable framework which allows infants to grow and learn in a secure interpersonal world.

SHARE YOUR PROSOCIAL VALUES CLEARLY

Photo: Nancy P. Alexander

Firm adult messages teach children social values.

Research on the early development of concern for others has revealed how important parental values are for the development of altruism. Parents who firmly tell and show their babies that they will not accept hurting actions as a way to solve social conflicts are more likely to have infants and toddlers who express concern when others are hurt or upset. Parents of altruistic babies also modelled generous soothing and comforting behaviors if their own babies were frightened by a barking dog or hurt after a fall.

When caregivers express firmly and clearly that they value considerate, nurturing behaviors and do not tolerate hitting or hurting others, then very young children internalize these values early and thoroughly. Reserve a clear "NO!" for important rules about unacceptable behaviors, such as "You must not hurt another person. I cannot allow you to hit. I will protect you so nobody hits you!"

Firm messages expressing adult values in favor of prosocial rather than aggressive ways to resolve social issues will increase positive interactions among even very young toddlers.

Overly permissive adults do not serve infants' interests well. When caregivers allow hurting to go on in a childcare setting by ignoring children who physically assault others, they are signalling their approval.

Toddlers are quite sensitive to adult cues of approval or disapproval of social actions. They are also sensitive to trust issues. If you promise a toddler in group care that she can have a turn on the new tricycle after Rondell has had his five minute ride, then be sure to follow through. Go and get Tara on the playground and remind her of your promise; give her a turn with the tricycle. Toddlers may forget temporarily, but they do learn to trust adults who consistently keep their promises. Your consistency can lead to many positive social interactions such as fewer fights over new toys or fewer aggressive reactions when asked to share. By keeping your promises, you can increase a child's trustfulness in the classroom and the home.

OFFER ALTERNATIVES TO UNACCEPTABLE BEHAVIORS

Babies are budding young scientists. They taste, pull, poke, wave, and bang to find out about objects, toys, foods. They squeeze bananas through their fingers. They drop food from a high chair table and peer over the edge with keen interest to see where the food fell. At about 10 months, a child may pull off a caregiver's eyeglasses over and over. Such experiments are

Photo: Francis Wardle

Offer alternatives that help young children experience objects.

not deliberate naughty behaviors. They are explorations. However, if adults feel that some baby explorations require too much clean up, they need to offer alternatives. The baby **can** toss yarn balls but not food. The baby **can** squeeze nubby plastic balls but not squeeze skin on another baby. The baby may bite a teething ring but not a peer.

Offering alternatives that satisfy an infant's needs to experience objects and persons physically requires much creative planning from a caregiver. Decide what the baby is trying to learn and arrange learning experiences that do not involve as much

42

mess or as much danger as exploratory biting, for example. If a toddler needs to spit, tell him "You may spit in the toilet. You really needed to spit. You cannot spit at a person. That hurts a person's feelings. You may spit in the toilet. Spit again. You can spit in the toilet bowl or in the sink." This satiation technique actually may result in the child's feeling that he has had quite enough of spitting and feels his mouth getting dry! Negative anger and punishment would only suppress the behavior but not channel it within acceptable, strictly limited boundaries. Nor would the toddler learn WHY such assaulting behavior is totally inappropriate.

Biting is a problem in group care settings. Be sure each infant gets enough personalized attention and has enough experiences sucking. Offer a teething object to a baby who needs to bite. People are not for biting, rubber teething rings are!

USE HUMOR

A smile, a grin, a tickly burble of your lips on a bare tummy, a funny face as you wrinkle your

Photo: Subjects and Predicates
Humor will increase positive attitudes.

nose, all are ways to lighten a situation when a toddler is acting somewhat rambunctious. Cheerfully call out to the toddler who is gleefully run-run-running away crowing "NO, NO, NO" right after you have called her for lunch: "Shoshannah, we are having baseballs with ketchup for lunch and sand pies for dessert, lovey." Such absurd talk may set a toddler giggling and turning around to race back toward the dining area. Stern, overexaggerated adult responses to a child's minor misdemeanors or feisty assertions of individuality often lead to resentments, tears, and bewildered babies.

Sometimes silly talk, or grinning toddler-level "jokes" can often ease a situation back into a cooperative mode. Humor will increase positive toddler approach to foods. "I'm a bunny rabbit going crunch, crunch, crunch," the caregiver remarks while exaggerating her chewing motions

with carrot sticks left over in a basket on the lunch
table. Despite the fact that the toddlers have
"finished" their lunch, each one then grabs a carrot
stick and crunches down the vegetable while
grinning broadly. Coercing children to eat does not
guarantee their love of a varied diet. Using humor is
far more effective than scolding.

Jenny was crawling up the front hall stairs.
Practicing her new found, exhilarating skills, she
launched herself into climbing mode over and over
again, even though her father scooped her back
down after every effort. Finally, without spanking or
scolding, her father decided to teach Jenny how to
climb up the stairs on four paws, and then come
down backwards safely. "Tush first," Papa called
out gaily (using a familiar family word for her
backside) after Jenny had padded up a few steps.
Soon, she was giggling at his cheerful reminder. A
bit later, she was even remembering to swivel
herself to go down backwards after creeping up a
few steps. Her father's humorous approach avoided
a struggle of wills as Jenny persistently worked at
mastering a fascinating new skill.

VARY THE TEMPO OF ACTIVITIES AND DAYS

Vary the types of activities used with young children

Photo: Nancy P. Alexander

Babies and toddlers tire easily. What was a fun game a few moments ago now evokes cranky or avoidant responses. Adults need to vary the rhythms of activities and days for little ones. Alternate quiet times with more busy or noisy times. After a bout of vigorous play or circle galloping, arrange for some peaceful sit-down activities, such as vanilla pudding finger painting. If toddlers have been playing at sedentary games for a long while, lure them into using their large muscles more for a while. Be alert to signs of fatigue. Be careful to ease transitions so that becoming overly tired is avoided.

Low lights and low voices signal that a wind-down time is approaching. Talk about "inside voices" and "outside voices" so little ones learn that shouting is not appropriate inside but is part of outdoor play as they run around the playground.

REFOCUS AND REDIRECT INAPPROPRIATE ACTIONS. LURE BABIES INTO APPROPRIATE ACTIVITIES.

Babies will attend to objects and people that attract their attention.

Toddlers are not yet sophisticated in their thinking. They are just beginning to learn that the feelings and thoughts of others may be different from their own. They have short attention spans. Instead of getting into a wrestling match verbally in order to get a toddler to cease and desist from an unwanted behavior, it may be easier simply to distract the child. Suppose that with unsteady gait 15-month-old James is pursuing Billy with a rubber toy bat upraised to bop Billy. Whirl James up into your arms with a hug and redirect him to banging on a peg board set where he can hammer pegs while sitting sociably next to Doreen, who is busy hammering too.

Lure a very young child into another interesting activity if the activity she is engaged in is getting too fractious or leading to frayed tempers. If another child needs a turn at a given activity, such as the water play table, remind the children about turn-taking. You may need to restate fairly often the rule about taking turns. Lure a child into another interesting activity through orienting the child with words. Point out other toddlers engaged happily in another activity. Luring works well; it allows the toddler to disengage from the current activity to go with you and begin to participate in a different type of play or new activity.

RESPECT INDIVIDUAL TEMPERAMENT STYLES

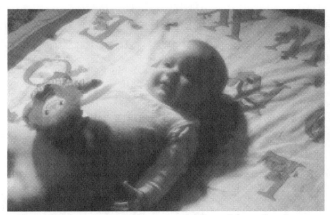

Easy babies approach new activities with enthusiasm.

Infants are born with varying temperament styles. Adults need to discipline each child with respect for and sensitivity to his temperament style. Some babies are easier to care for. *Easy babies* have upbeat moods, and are rhythmic in their bodily functions such as sleeping or voiding. *Easy babies* approach new possibilities for play, or new persons, with enthusiasm and positive adaptation.

Other babies are born with a more *difficult temperament*. Negative in mood, they may react to hunger pangs, wet diapers, or new foods with strong protest and intense crying. They may void or sleep with irregular patterns that are hard to predict. The child with *difficult temperament* needs your reassuring, authoritative presence. Repeat rules in a firm voice. If Andy snatches Maija's doll, state calmly: "Maija is taking care of her baby doll now. She needs it. She doesn't want you to grab it. Come, I will help you find another doll to play with."

Irritable babies who feel well loved grow up just as likely to be securely attached to their caregivers as easy babies. Feeling cherished by an adult who consistently uses a firm and calm approach makes all the difference.

A third group of babies are referred to as *slow-to-warm-up*. They are suspicious or fearful of new foods, caregivers, and situations. They have low-key moods and need more time to adjust to new environments or routines. The *slow-to-warm-up* baby needs to be introduced slowly to a new activity. She needs a caregiver to hold her hand as she eases into the sandbox, gets acquainted with the pail and shovel, and experiences the feel of sand on her fingers. The *slow-to-warm-up* baby will need extra help in meeting new people and experiencing things that she has not seen or heard before.

OFFER CLEAR CHOICES ACCEPTABLE TO YOU

Many toddlers respond with the familiar word "No" even to mild or reasonable adult requests. For example, ask a toddler if she wants juice; she may answer "No!". And you may get the same answer if you then ask "Do you want milk?" However, if you frame the question offering a *choice,* a toddler feels she has power. She can decide. So if the adult next asks, "Which do you want Tanya, juice or milk?" The toddler may cheerfully and firmly select a drink.

Photo: Nancy P. Alexander

Offer choices—children need a say in their lives.

A toddler whom caregivers had much difficulty in settling at nap time was asked finally one day: "Tamar, which side of the cot do you want to put your head down on . . . this side or that side?" Usually nagged by adults at nap time, the toddler considered both options, then decided and firmly pointed "This side." "Good choice" affirmed the caregiver, as she helped Tamar settle down peacefully for a nap for the first time in weeks. Toddlers need to feel they have a say in their lives. They have limited control over sphincters and over articulation of consonants. But caregivers who are perceptive will find ways to offer simple choices in appropriate creative ways. When toddlers feel that they have more control in a situation then they behave more compliantly with adult rules, such as napping or having a drink with a meal.

FRAME REQUESTS POSITIVELY

Many caregivers use "don't" or "quit that" too frequently. Toddlers then respond to the urgent and salient verb that follows the negative command. One day, two boys were running rather fast down a spiral path in an arboretum. The mother called out: "Don't run boys!" Hearing the word "RUN" loud and clear, both boys began to run even faster! Frame your requests for more appropriate behaviors in positive terms. Positive requests give a baby clues as to what you expect. Negative commands often impel a toddler to carry out the very action you disapprove of most!

For example:

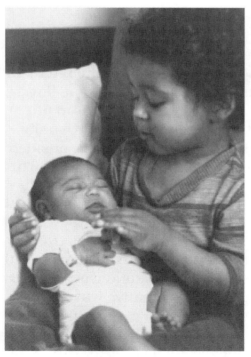

Photos: Francis Wardle

"Hold Angela gently, Jose. She likes it when you hold her gently."

"Walk slowly, Naffy. This is a steep driveway. You need to walk slowly and carefully."

"Hold the ball at the bottom, Danny. Then it will not fall on your foot."

SING SONGS AND CHANTS TO BOOST COOPERATION

Songs and rhythmic chants make transition times go more smoothly. Babies often have trouble changing from one activity to another. Chant on a few tones: "Soon it will be time for lunch. Soon we will clean up our toys. Soon we will have our lunch time." Infants and toddlers respond to rhythms and can bounce to rhythms by eight months of age. Songs are often a good way to make routines go easier. "This is the way we brush our teeth, brush our teeth, brush our teeth" makes tooth brushing more bearable and makes it easier for a squirming toddler to stand still as you brush her teeth.

Photo: Subjects and Predicates
Children respond well to rhythm and music.

Sing made-up songs with a child's name woven into the pattern of your words in order to alert the child to pay attention and get used to what will happen next. Miss Alice chanted in low tones: "Natalie Bess is waking up. Soon I will change Natalie's diapers. Soon she will come out of her crib. Natalie Bess is finishing her nap time." Hearing her name mentioned over and over, the baby quieted. She wanted to listen for her name mentioned in the caregiver's chant. Some babies wake up disoriented and upset from nap time. They may not remember that they are in a group care setting. They want mamma or papa to come and pick them up and cuddle them or change their diaper. Songs and chants are particularly useful in easing a baby's transition into childcare and the world of new adults.

GIVE TODDLERS WORDS TO EXPRESS EMOTIONS

Mad, sad, and *glad* are three words toddlers can learn to say. They are emotions every toddler has experienced. Give toddlers the words that allow them the power to communicate with adults when they are having strong positive or negative emotions. As children grow, give them new emotion words, such as *worried* or *puzzled*, *scared* or *happy*. Encourage young children to use these emotional words to tell you about their feelings. Toddlers

Photo: Francis Wardle
Help children express emotions with words.

will feel more able to ask for their needs to be met if they can communicate their emotions to adults. They will be less likely to act out bad/mad feelings if they can shout them out and enlist a caregiver's assistance for their problem.

Toddlers have strong wishes. Say "You *wish* you could have two ice creams just before dinner," or "You wish Jimmy were finished riding on the red tricycle this minute." Use the *"YOU WISH"* technique to let young children know that you understand their strong emotional wants. You are aware of the impulsive need to have their wishes come true right away. But using words to help children see causal connections (such as being too full to eat all their dinner if ice cream is the first large course) enlists their growing cognitive ability to reason. You confirm that they are important little persons as well. You value interpersonal sharing of rules and reasons with them even as you use words to acknowledge their strong wishes.

CHOOSE BOOKS FOR BIBLIOTHERAPY

Books help young children learn positive social behaviors.

Bibliotherapy means that we try to help little people learn to care and share by reading them books where the characters are nurturing and kind. Choose books for young children that will help them learn positive interpersonal social behaviors. *The Two Friends*, recounts the simple tale of Duck and Bear who are friends. Bear bakes delicious edibles. Duck is a neat housekeeper. Bear's kitchen is so messy that Duck sometimes gets her webbed feet stuck in all the glop on Bear's floor when he is busy cooking. One morning the two friends each secretly decide to express their caring for each other. At the very same time that Duck sets off to clean up Bear's house and make it nice and neat for him, his friend Bear, who woke up early to bake a surprise, is busy walking to Duck's house to bring a big platter of freshly baked cookies. Helpfulness, kindness, prosocial activities, such as turn taking, sharing, and comforting, can be learned by toddlers who love to listen to stories of good deeds over and over.

For example, Madeleine, a gifted and skillful caregiver, was reading *The Little Engine That Could*. In the story, a small blue train tries mightily and succeeds in chugging over a tall mountain in order to bring toys to children who live on the other side. The selfish big silver engine would not even try to make that trip. As Madeleine read, an older toddler, listening intently to the story of the courageous little blue engine, kept nodding and whispering to himself "That was very nice of her. That was very nice of her!" Enhance toddler appreciation of prosocial interactions through judicious choice of prosocial story and picture books to read to them.

TRANSFORM TIME-OUT TO A TEACH-IN TIME

Many adults send children to "time-out" or say "go to your room" as their preferred method of discipline. The adult is angry.

Photo: Nancy P. Alexander

Use time-out sparingly.

The child may well need to cool off from the overexcitement that led to a hurting or an inappropriate, disobedient, or defiant behavior. Time-out can be misused. It can be overused. When used to help children calm themselves until they feel ready to join a family or group care activity and interact according to group rules, time-out can be effective. It gives a child time to gather positive self control in order to function well again among other children and adults. Time-out as an unthinking technique is not very useful. A toddler is short on skill and strong on will.

Toddlers may not remember rules or understand reasons for rules. Toddlers struggle with learning self control when their wishes are strong and their sharing skills and frustration-coping skills are emerging. Adults who use time-out in conjunction with reminders about rules will be teaching a toddler rather than mindlessly applying a technique.

Use time-out sparingly. If a child is filled with rage and resentment, time-out is a poor discipline choice. One toddler, with very inconsistent experiences of parental discipline, urinated all over the time-out space, including cot and wooden screen, when he was placed there for three minutes by his childcare teacher. That child needed teachers to use more creativity in determining discipline methods to help him gain self control. Actually, wearing his favorite teacher's tie for a few hours was so important to him, that this child learned to control aggressive behaviors toward the toddlers in his group. He adored Mr. Galen and would try hard to control aggressive responses if he were allowed to wear Mr. Galen's tie. For him, time-out evoked feelings of mutual misunderstandings and of being abandoned psychologically.

Time-out does not work for every child or on every occasion. Be aware when one child is picked out for too much time-out. When a child experiences time out too frequently, more nurturing techniques or talking it over is more effective, especially in terms of long term compliance and cooperative behavior.

EXPLAIN THE CONSEQUENCES OF DANGEROUS BEHAVIORS

Photo: Nancy P. Alexander

Explain the consequences of dangerous behaviors.

As toddlers develop more verbal skills and thinking ability, add more simple explanations to your clear rules to keep little ones safe and healthy. Explain dangers simply but vividly. Cars go fast and can crush a person they smash into. Fire is very hot and burns; so, we must be careful not to touch any flame. We need to brush teeth or bad bacteria will make tiny holes in our teeth. Two-year-olds do not have to understand molecular biology. They can understand that bad microbes and germs make a person sick; hand washing before eating is a good rule because clean hands will keep bad germs from getting inside our bodies and making us sick.

TEACH TODDLERS TO USE WORDS NOT FISTS

Photo: Francis Wardle

Words are more effective than fists.

Give children words to use to help them solve social problems. If a child tries to snatch Tommy's toy, Tommy doesn't have to scream or smack the other toddler. He can use words loud and clear: "My toy!" He warns a peer loudly as he holds on to the toy. Other expressions, for taking turns, for explaining that one child needs a certain object, for offering to play together, are useful for toddlers just beginning to put two and three word phrases together. Role play these expressions. By providing words, you give toddlers a chance to learn how to get their needs met socially through the use of language rather than disapproved-of hurtful physical actions. Urge little ones to "use your words" instead of kicks, bites, or hits in response to interpersonal upsets. Refresh your toddlers' memories often: "Remember, use your words!"

BUILD SELF ESTEEM IN CHILDREN

Hugs, kisses, cuddles, responsive care, and love words are psychological vitamins that build children's self esteem. Shining adult eyes that show admiration and approval of new infant venturing, explorations, and early learning enhance children's self esteem.

Photo: Francis Wardle

Help children feel good about themselves.

Make lap time and hugging time generously available for babies who need psychological refueling, or for toddlers fatigued by practicing new skills. If a toddler tries to build a tall block tower with strenuous concentration and it suddenly topples, that toddler may need time on your lap to recover courage and zestfulness to try again. A child's courage to persevere in learning grows from the certainty of unconditional approval of his/her personhood and the bodily as well as the emotional availability of loving caregivers. Shame and ridicule are emotional acids that eat away at and destroy children's self esteem. Nourish the self esteem of young children so that discipline techniques will need to be used less often. Then when you do use them, infants and toddlers will be more likely to cooperate.

REFERENCES

Briggs, D. (1975). *Your child's self esteem*. New York: Dolphin.

Honig, A. S. (1982). *Playtime learning games for young children*. Syracuse, NY: Syracuse University Press.

Honig, A. S. (1992). Dancing with your baby means sometimes leading, sometimes following. *Dimensions of Early Childhood*, 20(2), 10-13.

Honig, A. S. (1995). Singing with infants and toddlers. *Young Children*, 50(5), 72-78.

Honig, A. S., & Brophy, H. E. (1996). *Talking with your baby: Family as the first school*. Syracuse, NY: Syracuse University Press.

Honig A. S., & Wittmer, D. S. (1988). Guidance: Vision Statement. In California State Department of Education (Ed.) *Visions for infant/toddler care: Guidelines for professional caregiving*, (62-80). Sacramento, CA, CSDE.

Stone, J. (1983). *A guide to discipline (rev.ed.)*. Washington, D.C.: National Association for the Education of Young Children.

SECA PUBLICATIONS

Outdoor Play For Infants and Toddlers

Suzanne Winter, Ph.D.
This newest book in the SECA publications department includes B & W photographs. How to design playgrounds for infants and toddlers. Safety guidelines and suggestions for outdoor activities for infants and toddlers.
30 pages.1995.
$3.00 for SECA members
$4.00 for others

Caring for Infants and Toddlers With Special Needs

Staisey Hodge, M.Ed.
An introduction to disabilities, special equipment, activities, communication, and colaboration with other professionals. Includes reproducible letter to parents.
30 pages.1995
$3.00 for SECA Members
$4.00 for others

Behavior Guidance for Three- and Four-year-old Children

Jeanette C. Nunnelley, Ed.D.
Why children misbehave, modeling, indirect and direct guidance techniques, realistic expectations, plus a guidance analysis form.
1995
$5.00 for SECA members
$6.00 for others

Legislative Platform for Children

A SECA position statement.
1995
$.40 for SECA members
$.50 for others

Special *Dimensions in Early Childhood* Reprint Series:

Literacy Development

Five articles dealing with helping young children explore the world of print, including tips for writing with children.
$2.00 for SECA members
$3.00 for others

Assessment

Five articles dealing with assessment of young children. Including Portifolio Based Assessment and Assessment of Social Development by Diane McClellan and Lilian Katz.
$2.00 for SECA members
$3.00 for others

Play

Five articles on both indoor and outdoor play. Featuring block play in the primary classroom and suggestions for problem solving in an outdoor play setting.
$2.00 for SECA members
$3.00 for others

Curriculum

Hands on math, touchable bulletin boards and multi-culturalism are addressed in this six article reprint series
$2.00 for SECA members
$3.00 for others

Trade Discount - 25%

Please add the following amounts for shipping and handling:
$2.00 for orders of up to $10.00;
$4.00 for orders of $10.01 to $20.00;
$5.00 for orders of $20.01 to $40.00;
$6.00 for orders of $40.01 to $60.00.

Send checks to **SECA, P.O. Box 55930, Little Rock, AR, 72215-5930.**